About Woodpeckers

A Guide for Children

Cathryn Sill

Illustrated by John Sill

PEACHTREE

ATLANTA

For the One who created woodpeckers.

—*Genesis* 1:25

Ω

Published by
PEACHTREE PUBLISHERS
1700 Chattahoochee Avenue
Atlanta, Georgia 30318-2112
www.peachtree-online.com

Edited by Vicky Holifield

Illustrations created in watercolor on archival quality 100% rag watercolor paper
Text and titles typeset in Novarese from Adobe Systems

Printed in May 2018 by Imago in China
10 9 8 7 6 5 4 3 2 1
First Edition

ISBN 978-1-68263-004-4

Library of Congress Cataloging-in-Publication Data

Names: Sill, Cathryn P., 1953- author. | Sill, John, illustrator.
Title: About woodpeckers : a guide for children / written by Cathryn Sill ; illustrated by John Sill.
Description: First edition. | Atlanta : Peachtree Publishers, [2018] | Audience: Ages 3-7. | Audience: Grade K to 3.
Identifiers: LCCN 2017023858 | ISBN 9781682630044
Subjects: LCSH: Woodpeckers—Juvenile literature.
Classification: LCC QL696.P56 S55 2018 | DDC 598.7/2—dc23 LC record available at *https://lccn.loc.gov/2017023858*

About Woodpeckers

Woodpeckers are birds with strong, sharp bills used for drilling and pecking.

PLATE 1
Cream-colored Woodpecker

Powerful neck muscles and thick skulls allow woodpeckers to pound again and again without hurting themselves.

PLATE 2
Black Woodpecker

Woodpeckers have small feathers covering their nostrils. These feathers keep out the sawdust when the woodpeckers drill into trees.

PLATE 3
Downy Woodpecker

They often talk to one another by drumming on a hard surface with their bills.

PLATE 4
White-browed Piculet

Most woodpeckers live where trees grow.

PLATE 5
Red-headed Woodpecker

A few live in other places.

PLATE 6
a. **Gilded Flicker**
b. **Ground Woodpeckers**
c. **Bamboo Woodpecker**

a.
c.
b.

Woodpeckers have strong feet and sharp claws that help them climb.

PLATE 7
White Woodpecker

Their stiff tail feathers hold them up as they prop themselves or move along the trunks of trees.

PLATE 8
Black-headed Woodpecker

Woodpeckers drill holes for nests and for sleeping.

PLATE 9
Great Spotted Woodpecker

Some make small holes for storing food.

PLATE 10
Acorn Woodpecker

Many other animals use woodpecker holes.

PLATE 11
Northern Flying Squirrel

Woodpeckers hunt for food by pecking.
They eat mostly insects.

PLATE 12
Common Flameback

They also eat fruits, nuts, and seeds.

PLATE 13
Yellow-fronted Woodpecker

A few eat tree sap.

PLATE 14
Williamson's Sapsucker

Woodpeckers use their long, sharp tongues
to help them get food.

PLATE 15
Eurasian Green Woodpecker

Sometimes woodpeckers drill into the wood on houses or buildings. The holes they make can cause problems for people.

PLATE 16
Northern Flicker

Woodpeckers help forests by eating many insects that harm trees.

PLATE 17
Pileated Woodpecker

It is important to protect woodpeckers and the places where they live.

PLATE 18
Okinawa Woodpecker

Afterword

PLATE 1
There are more than two hundred species of woodpeckers in the world. These birds live in wooded habitats on all the continents except Australia-Oceania and Antarctica. Most species of woodpeckers inhabit lowland tropical rainforests. Cream-colored Woodpeckers live in humid forests in parts of South America.

PLATE 2
Woodpeckers peck eight to twelve thousand times each day. They have a spongy cushion in their head that protects their brain. Black Woodpeckers have a strong, slender neck that allows them to dig deep holes in trees. They live in much of Europe and parts of Asia.

PLATE 3
Woodpeckers have small feathers called "nasal tufts" covering their nostrils. These feathers keep out the sawdust when the woodpeckers drill into trees. Downy Woodpeckers have pale nasal tufts on top of their dark bill. They are the smallest woodpecker in North America.

PLATE 4
Woodpeckers drum on hard surfaces to attract a mate, to defend their territory, and sometimes to warn others of danger. They can hit a tree with their bill up to twenty times a second. Woodpeckers do not sing like other birds. They use their voices to call to each other with chirps, chatters, and rattles. White-browed Piculets drum loudly on bamboo (a giant, woody grass). They live in Southeast Asia.

PLATE 5
Many woodpeckers live in heavily forested areas. Others live at forest edges and places where the trees are farther apart. Red-headed Woodpeckers live in open, sunny woodlands in eastern and central North America.

PLATE 6
Woodpeckers that live in deserts often excavate holes in large cactuses such as saguaros. Gilded Flickers live in the southwestern United States and northwestern Mexico. Ground Woodpeckers make holes in banks and steep slopes. They live in southern Africa. As their name suggests, Bamboo Woodpeckers live mainly in stands of bamboo that grow in forests in parts of Southeast Asia.

PLATE 7
Most woodpeckers have zygodactyl feet, which means each foot has two toes pointing forward and two toes pointing backward. Long claws help them cling to the side of a tree as they drill and hunt for food. White Woodpeckers hop on tree trunks in noisy family groups. They live in South America, east of the Andes Mountains.

PLATE 8
The long, stiff tail feathers of woodpeckers give them extra support as they climb up and cling to trees. They rarely climb down. Black-headed Woodpeckers move from tree to tree looking for food at all levels, from the ground to the treetops. They live in Southeast Asia.

PLATE 9
Many types of woodpeckers use dead or dying trees for their holes or cavities. Others choose to drill into the softer wood of dead limbs on a healthy tree. This makes it easier for them to excavate the cavity. Great Spotted Woodpeckers usually build a new nest hole each year. They are common and widespread across much of Eurasia and in parts of North Africa.

PLATE 10

Trees used for food storage by woodpeckers are called "granary trees." Some woodpeckers store food in cracks in the bark or in other available holes. Acorn Woodpeckers drill thousands of holes that are just the right size for one acorn. They will defend their food stores from other animals that might try to rob them. Acorn Woodpeckers live in the western United States and Central America.

PLATE 11

Many small animals, including birds and mammals, need cavities to live in. They often use abandoned woodpecker holes. Northern Flying Squirrels use woodpecker holes for shelter in winter. Often several flying squirrels will curl up together in a hole to stay warm. Northern Flying Squirrels are found in Canada and parts of the United States.

PLATE 12

Many woodpeckers peck holes in wood, looking for insects. Others peel away the tree bark and search for food in cracks and crevices. Some species of woodpeckers raid ant or termite nests on the ground. Several kinds of woodpeckers catch flying insects. Common Flamebacks live in Southeast Asia. They sometimes eat small scorpions as well as insects.

PLATE 13
Woodpeckers depend on foods that are available each season. Those that live in places with cold winters must be able to find things to eat when insects are scarce. Many of them stash food to eat later. Tropical woodpeckers do not need to store as much food. Yellow-fronted Woodpeckers eat a lot of fruit. They live in rainforests in eastern South America.

PLATE 14
Some kinds of woodpeckers drill small holes in trees so that sap oozes out. Sapsuckers have a brushy tip on their tongue that helps them lick up the sticky liquid. They also eat insects that are attracted to the sap. Williamson's Sapsuckers live in western North America.

PLATE 15
Each kind of woodpecker has a distinctive type of tongue that helps it get the food it needs. Many woodpeckers have a sharp, barbed tongue that they use as a spear. Others use their tongue to rake the food toward their mouth. Some, such as the Eurasian Green Woodpecker, have a sticky tongue that can be used to pull insects from holes. Eurasian Green Woodpeckers often look for food on the ground. They live in Europe and western Asia.

PLATE 16

When woodpeckers peck holes in buildings or wooden utility poles, people consider them to be pests. Some people are disturbed by the noise they make by drumming on houses or gutters. Woodpeckers eating crops can cause problems for fruit and nut farmers. Northern Flickers sometimes annoy homeowners with their loud hammering. They are widespread in North America.

PLATE 17

Woodpeckers control many insects that destroy trees in forests all over the world. The holes woodpeckers make provide homes for animals that are not able to dig their own. Many people enjoy watching woodpeckers. Pileated Woodpeckers excavate large holes in dead wood as they look for food. Other birds are also able to find food where Pileated Woodpeckers have been feeding. Pileateds live in North America, in forests with large trees.

PLATE 18

We can help woodpeckers that live near us by leaving dead trees and snags that are not dangerous to people or buildings. The presence of woodpeckers is one sign that a forest is healthy. Logging and clearing forests for reasons such as development or farming should be done in a way that protects woodpeckers and the other wildlife that lives there. Okinawa Woodpeckers are one of the rarest woodpeckers in the world. They are critically endangered because their habitat has been destroyed. Okinawa Woodpeckers now live only in a very small part of Japan.

GLOSSARY

cavity—a hole or hollow place
excavate—to make a hole by digging
habitat—the place where animals and plants live and grow
humid—wet, damp; having a lot of water vapor in the air
sap—a liquid that flows through a plant
species—a group of animals or plants that are alike in many ways
tropical—hot year-round

SUGGESTIONS FOR FURTHER READING

Books

Amazing Animals: Woodpeckers by Kate Riggs (Creative Education, Creative Paperbacks)
Woodpecker Wham! by April Pulley Sayre (Henry Holt and Co.)

Websites

www.defenders.org/woodpeckers/basic-facts
birding.about.com/od/birdprofiles/a/15-Fun-Facts-About-Woodpeckers.htm
www.listverse.com/2015/07/12/10-weird-and-wonderful-facts-about-woodpeckers
blog.nwf.org/2014/12/8-wonky-and-wonderful-woodpecker-adaptations

RESOURCES ESPECIALLY HELPFUL IN DEVELOPING THIS BOOK

Woodpeckers of the World: A Photographic Guide by Gerard Gorman (Firefly Books)
Peterson Reference Guide to Woodpeckers of North America by Stephen A. Shunk (Houghton Mifflin Harcourt)

ABOUT... SERIES

978-1-68263-031-0 HC
978-1-68263-032-7 PB

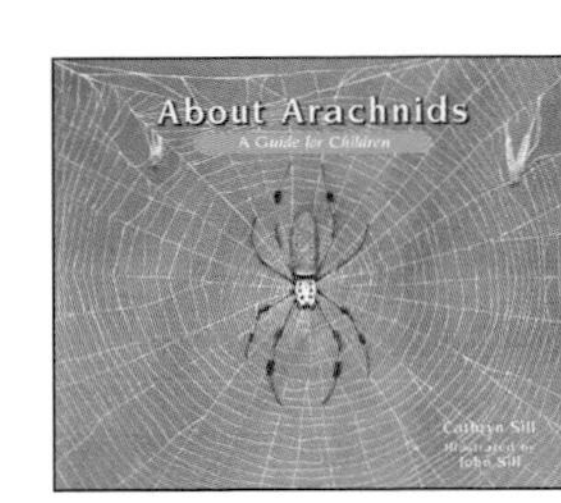

978-1-56145-038-1 HC
978-1-56145-364-1 PB

978-1-56145-688-8 HC
978-1-56145-699-4 PB

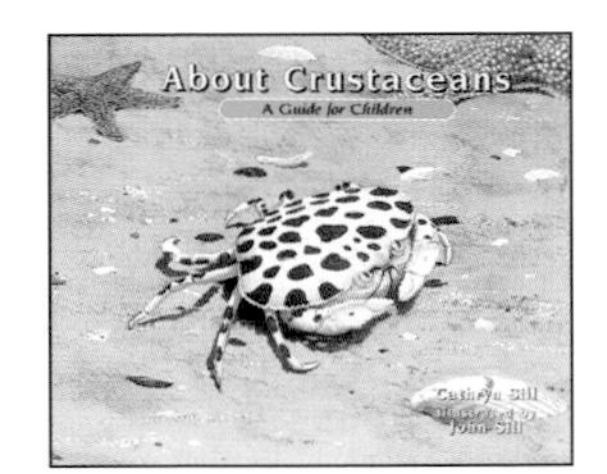

978-1-56145-301-6 HC
978-1-56145-405-1 PB

978-1-56145-987-2 HC
978-1-56145-988-9 PB

978-1-56145-588-1 HC
978-1-56145-837-0 PB

978-1-56145-881-3 HC
978-1-56145-882-0 PB

978-1-56145-757-1 HC
978-1-56145-758-8 PB

978-1-56145-906-3 HC

978-1-56145-358-0 HC
978-1-56145-407-5 PB

978-1-56145-331-3 HC
978-1-56145-406-8 PB

978-1-56145-795-3 HC

978-1-56145-743-4 HC
978-1-56145-741-0 PB

978-1-56145-536-2 HC
978-1-56145-811-0 PB

978-1-56145-907-0 HC
978-1-56145-908-7 PB

978-1-56145-454-9 HC
978-1-56145-914-8 PB

- About Birds / *Sobre los pájaros* / 978-1-56145-783-0 PB • About Mammals / *Sobre los mamíferos* / 978-1-56145-800-4 PB
- About Insects / *Sobre los insectos* / 978-1-56145-883-7 PB • About Reptiles / *Sobre los reptiles* / 978-1-56145-909-4 PB
- About Fish / *Sobre los peces* / 978-1-56145-989-6 PB • About Amphibians / *Sobre los anfibios* / 978-1-68263-033-4 PB

About Habitats series

978-1-56145-641-3 HC
978-1-56145-636-9 PB

978-1-56145-734-2 HC

978-1-56145-559-1 HC
978-1-68263-034-1 PB

978-1-56145-469-3 HC
978-1-56145-731-1 PB

978-1-56145-618-5 HC
978-1-56145-960-5 PB

978-1-56145-832-5 HC

978-1-56145-432-7 HC
978-1-56145-689-5 PB

978-1-56145-968-1 HC

The Sills

CATHRYN AND JOHN SILL are the dynamic team who created the *About...* series as well as the *About Habitats* series. Their books have garnered praise from educators and have won a variety of awards, including Bank Street Best Books, CCBC Choices, NSTA/CBC Outstanding Science Trade Books for Students K–12, Orbis Pictus Recommended, and *Science Books and Films* Best Books of the Year. Cathryn, a graduate of Western Carolina State University, taught early elementary school classes for thirty years. John holds a BS in wildlife biology from North Carolina State University. Combining his artistic skill and knowledge of wildlife, he has achieved an impressive reputation as a wildlife artist. The Sills live in Franklin, North Carolina.

Fred Eldredge, Creative Image Photography